Mission and Money

Funding Christian mission

by Stewardship Services

kitab
Interserve resources

Published by Kitab – Interserve Resources

5/6 Walker Avenue

Wolverton Mill

Milton Keynes

MK12 5TW

t. 01908 552700

e. kitab@isewi.org

w. www.kitab.org.uk

Stewardship Services

PO Box 99, Loughton, Essex IG10 3QJ

t. 020 8502 8585

f. 020 8502 5333

e. education@stewardship.org.uk

w. www.stewardship.org.uk

Stewardship is the operating name of Stewardship Services (UKET) Limited, a registered charity no. 234714, and a company limited by guarantee no. 90305, registered in England

Contents

Acknowledgement

We at Interserve appreciate the contribution of Stewardship to the production of 'Mission and Money'.

The Interserve/Stewardship partnership to produce this booklet – from edit to final proof – has been vital to produce what you are holding in your hand. We believe it will be a foundational building block in your thinking about the "how" and "why" of funding mission.

Interserve would also like to thank Stephen Mathews from Stewardship, for his willingness to work closely with Interserve; then there are Fiona Mearns and Alan Hough who have offered guidance and steered the process to its conclusion.

We also acknowledge friend of Interserve Myles Wilson who is the source of much of our current thinking about money and which permeates much of the content of this book.

Alastair McIver
Head of Fundraising (Interserve)

Introduction

In booklet number 8 of this series, we explore the changing face of Christian mission. During the 1800s and 1900s, the mission enterprise was heavily influenced by the fact that Britain had an Empire. This opened up mission opportunities for, what became called 'Mission Societies'. These Societies took the gospel along trading routes, into the British colonies and outposts of the time.

This colonial arrangement has all but ended and new ways of doing Christian mission are emerging. The economics of Christian mission are also changing, so while the modern mission journey is still undertaken by individuals – they still tend to go through 'mission agencies' and are individually supported by their friends, family and other partners.

Today organisations such as *Stewardship* are facilitating a more personalised approach to the financial support of those engaged in Christian mission. This is the stuff of the future and so we at Interserve (a mission-sending fellowship) are delighted to be in a partner relationship with Stewardship, not only to commission this booklet but also to explore together the mechanism for money to enable mission in a future-friendly way.

Steve Bell
Series Editor

Where do I start?

Your story is unique. It belongs only to you and the way in which your story becomes part of God's bigger story is as individual as you are. However, the challenges you face as your story unfolds are not unique – they have been experienced by God's people since the very beginning and will continue to be experienced by other Christian workers across the world in a variety of situations and places.

This booklet aims to look at some of the issues which lie at the core of living on personal support so you can see them in a right perspective, avoiding becoming overshadowed by them, nor overlooking anything.

So how do we know about the challenges you face? Firstly, Interserve and Stewardship have been involved in facilitating and supporting mission since 1852 and 1906 respectively and we've listened to a lot of people's stories since then!

> Many mission workers are under financial pressure. I can't help thinking something is wrong.
> Survey Respondent

More recently, by means of a survey, Stewardship asked some direct questions to a sample group[1] of Christian workers, and what came back bore out much of what we suspected from anecdotal evidence: that money and the future featured as the main concern in ministry – causing sleepless nights for around a third of those responding; twice as many as any other type of concern. Concerns were not limited to the amount of money but extended to include a wide variety of other money-related issues in ministry.

However, most workers felt that they needed on average 25% more income than their current level in order to be at a 'suitable level' and what they thought was 'suitable' was below what we thought it should be! We'll be examining 'how much is enough' in chapter 5.

We also learned from these same responses, that there are common barriers which prevent

---

1   *Around 200 respondents*

Christian workers satisfactorily communicating with potential supporters and the most common of all were the barriers that come from within - embarrassment, feeling unable to express need, or feeling able to clearly communicate what their ministry is about. For some, the fundamental question 'is it right to ask?' lies at the heart of their dilemma and we explore this further in chapter 3.

For some, the tension between lack of funding and the inability to communicate their legitimate needs to potential supporters is very great and it can affect both their work and their relationships. The physical distance from their supporters can be a literal barrier to effective communication and there are often cross-cultural issues, which affect how they communicate need. Returning to a home church after a period abroad can sometimes serve to highlight the different expectations in standards of living for example (see chapter 6).

Fear of rejection is a recurring and all too common theme for many workers and can inhibit approaches to new supporters. Even those that appear to find it 'easy' to approach potential supporters have moments when fear takes hold.

> I occasionally revert to a fearful mind-set but I am constantly surprised by the positive response I get.
> Training day delegate

Financial literacy can be a stumbling block for many. One finance manager for a mission organisation told us that one of the major problems he encountered with mission workers is a lack of basic finance management skills.

Another common issue is that of retirement and pensions. All too often Christian workers don't have enough pension-provision and have no idea what to do about it. Two thirds of those surveyed expected to receive a UK state pension eventually and yet nearly half said they either didn't pay or didn't know if they paid National Insurance contributions. See chapter 4, under 'financial responsibilities' for more details about thinking longer-term.

So what's the good news?! Firstly, that you have God on your side and where there is a clear call to overseas mission that He will help prepare the way in which it will be supported. Secondly, if you're reading this, you have an opportunity to equip yourself and prepare for what lies ahead. You'll know where to look for help and how to find out more about specific areas which may affect you financially. This isn't the last word on all matters financial but it is a good starting point.

We acknowledge that recognising and answering God's call rests at the heart of this step in your life and that money is certainly not the most crucial aspect of your ministry, but it is an important area and when not handled properly can be a drain on your fruitfulness. By upholding the value of good money management and realistic budgeting we aim to help you develop a healthy attitude towards money and its place in your ministry.

> I didn't realise when I started this work a year ago, how much I had to think about.
> Delegate at Christian Worker Training

One Bible college student said: *'We raised the funding by the goodness of God who has provided everything. How has He has done that by placing on the hearts of individuals and trusts, the desire to support us and our vision for ministry. This has also meant that we have needed to be careful to be good stewards of this financial support.'*

The final, and possibly most fundamental point to make is that our spiritual lives and our financial dealings are closely connected. The Bible contains over 2,000 verses on money which is more than on faith and prayer put together. Jesus constantly referred to financial matters in his parables and the way in which we handle money is a key indicator of our spiritual health. So, far from money being seen as a necessary evil to finance ministry, it is an intrinsic part of it. We look further at the biblical basis for living on support in the next section and also how God's provision creates a new dynamic in different groups of people.

For reflection and/or discussion on Chapter 1

1. Reflect on the fact that your journey in mission has aspects that are totally unique to you.
2. Reflect on the fact that the Bible has over 2,000 verses about money (i.e. more than faith and prayer put together) and that Jesus used financial matters as a key indicator of spiritual health. So far from money being a 'necessary evil', it is an intrinsic part of your ministry.

Questions

1. Although your experience is unique, what do you share with all those who have gone before you – including Bible characters?
2. Where does money feature in your list of concerns about full-time ministry – does it cause you sleepless nights or does it excite you?
3. How would you rate your level of financial acumen on a scale of 1-5?

Notes

God is the Provider

Jehovah Jireh

In Numbers 18 we read about the very first structured support system, introduced to allow the Levites to work full-time in the Tabernacle (see section below, *Living on support - a biblical Heritage*). To do this, God arranged for them not to inherit any territory in the Promised Land. This way, they wouldn't be distracted from serving God by needing to earn a normal income. Instead they were to be funded by the tithes from the rest of the people.

> *"You will have no inheritance in their land, nor will you have any share among them; I am your share and your inheritance among the Israelites. I give to the Levites all the tithes in Israel as their inheritance in return for the work they do while serving at the Tent of Meeting."* (Nums.18:20-21)

I now see giving and receiving as a kind of "spiritual correspondence".

A mission worker

Although the money to support the Levites was given by the rest of the people, God stresses in the passage that He is the provider, not the givers. When we live on personal support, although the money comes from the hands (or, more often, bank accounts) of our friends, churches and contacts, we must never lose sight of the fact that God is the provider, not supporters. Those who send are following a call of God on their lives to do so. Those who go are doing likewise.

Some time later in their history, the people of Israel turned away from God and then, under the influence of King Hezekiah, turned back to Him and recommenced their giving. This resulted in surplus and a sub-committee was set up to decide how to use these extra funds.

> *'And they distributed to the priests enrolled by their families in the genealogical records and likewise to the Levites twenty years old or more, according to their responsibilities and their divisions. They included all the little ones, the wives, and the sons and daughters of the whole community listed in these genealogical records. For they were faithful in consecrating themselves.'* (2 Chrons.31:12-18)

So God wasn't just paying the priests and Levites for the work they did serving him. He was setting up an economic system that took care of an entire family, even specifically showing care for the babies in the families. It was a system of provision that had a long-term aim and was offering care generation after generation.

For some, the tradition of serving God full-time while he provides for them through the gifts of the rest of his people continues to this day. It is a partnership of equals, those giving and sending fulfilling their call under God to do so; those receiving and going doing likewise. Paul understood this when he told his supporters in Philippi that he thanked God for their *"partnership in the gospel"* (Phils.1:5).

> All resources belong to God and he entrusts some of them to us. We are dependent on God's provision, whatever the actual immediate source of the money.

However, there is often a line of thinking that endows the gift of money from the supporter with 'ownership' rights. This can lead to supporters considering that they have a right to inspect the lifestyle and money-use of the mission partner to see how 'their' money is being used. But they would consider it close to an offence if the supporter had the same expectations and wanted to enquire into the lifestyle and money-use of the supporter!

In reality all the world's resources belong to God and he entrusts some of those resources to us for His glory and for the extension of His kingdom. So we are all dependent on God's provision, whatever the actual immediate source of the money.

Furthermore, we are all *'worthy of our hire'* (1Tim.5:18) whether working as a school teacher and receiving God's provision through the country's tax system or working as a mission partner and receiving God's provision through the gifts of his people. In both cases our provision for our present and future needs is from God. It is easy for the supporter to see their salary as their provision and so miss the reality that God is their provider.

But it is equally as easy for mission workers to see their supporters as their provider and miss the reality too. In both cases it leads to a focus on a provider that isn't God, and a desire to work to please that provider (the employer in one case, the supporter on the other). That's close to the first steps on the road to idolatry and that's a dangerous road to go down.

Living on support - a biblical concept

Throughout history God has set apart specific people to be involved in aspects of ministry which mean they were not free to generate an income themselves so were supported by others. Today we tend to call this 'living on support', but it is a concept that has its origins in the scriptures.

The first example we see is in Numbers 18 (see section above, God the provider). In a society where land was at the heart of the economy, getting no land effectively meant getting no income. The Levites got the Promise of God's provision, but not the Land that they might have expected. And God's provision was dependent on the faithfulness of God's people in their giving. I wonder how the Levites felt about it?

Then in Luke 8:1-3 we read that Jesus and the disciples were supported by a group of women who had benefitted from Jesus' ministry. They were from a range of social backgrounds and would have been considered by the religious establishment as being, at best, on the fringes of faith. Yet these were the people who chose to support Jesus and he accepted their support.

Receiving can be a real problem for some who live on support, especially when the giver is less well-off than the receiver. Yet here we have the second person of the trinity, the person for whom and by whom everything was created, being willing to accept support. He could have commanded to be provided for supernaturally, but instead he chose to be provided for the same way you are – by the gifts of those committed to him and his ministry.

A little later we see Paul discussing his support with two churches in particular: first the Corinthians who chose not to support him (1Cors.9:2-14) and then the Philippians who did (Phils.4:10-20).

> While there is an element of being paid for what we do, there is also an element of being cared for by a loving Father.

With the Corinthians, Paul takes them to task for not supporting him, clearly annoyed and even upset with them (see 2 Cors.11:7-10;12:11-13). The issue, again, isn't whether or not he received, but in this case the lack of spiritual maturity in the Corinthians, which meant that they didn't give. His argument about support is part of a bigger discussion with them about the dangers of demanding their rights as Christians.

He tells them that he has the right to demand their support, but doesn't do so because they aren't mature enough to cope with this demand. But he does make it clear that the default position for those involved in Christian ministry is to be funded by God's people.

With the Philippians he was more excited that they gave, than that he received. He talks about their account getting credited (presumably their account in heaven, not in the Bank of Philippi!), describes their support as being a fragrant offering, an acceptable sacrifice, pleasing to God and tells them that God will meet all their needs (notice that this promise is for the supporter, not the receiver).

So living on a support basis is following a long biblical tradition. It is a calling from the God of the universe and, as such, is a massive privilege. Like everything else we receive from God, support is an act of grace and while there is an element of being paid for what we do, there is also an element of being cared for by a loving Father.

It might be seen as an unusual way of living and therefore might not always be understood by others. Also, because it depends on givers being faithful to God's call on their lives to give and receivers being faithful to God's call on their lives to serve him, there is always the risk that it won't work out as we'd like it to but it is the way God has set up for people to work full-time for him and be provided for. Welcome to this great heritage!

For more on this topic see chapter two in *Funding the Family Business*, available from www.ftfb.org

For reflection and/or discussion on Chapter 2

1. If Numbers 18 describes a clear structure for the financial support of people engaged in full-time ministry, reflect on what it might be about British culture that can cause us to be reticent about setting up such a structure.
2. How do you relate to the fact that God says he is the supplier behind the giving of the people?
3. Paul told his supporters in Philippi that he thanked God for their "partnership in the gospel" (Phils.1:5); what could you do to foster this kind of relationship with your supporters?

Questions

As a re-cap to help you remember, why not try to express (in one sentence for each), the system of personalised support practised by...

1. the Levites

2. Jesus

3. Paul – Corinth

4. Paul - Philippi

To ask or not to ask...that is the question

There is a question that often crops up during support raising seminars and it is this: "Is it okay to ask for support?" It comes in different forms, ranging from the theological: "is it biblical to ask?", to the emotional: "I'm too scared to ask, can't I just pray instead?" Interserve recognise the need to raise support and will help you through this process, but for some it will still not be easy because they retain the nagging thought: "Surely if I am doing God's will, He will provide all I need".

Was Hudson Taylor exercising more faith by not asking? Or was D.L. Moody showing more faith by approaching people for money?

Sometimes great heroes of the faith, like Hudson Taylor, get quoted as examples of people who didn't ask for support. Taylor said, "God's work, done God's way, will never lack God's supply". If they just prayed and didn't ask, the argument goes, then we shouldn't ask either. Sometimes this is described as living by faith.

But what about other great heroes of the faith who were equally used by God and who did ask? Like D.L. Moody, the American evangelist from the late 19th century who was hugely used by God in his day and who was very open about asking for money. He said: "I show my faith when I go to men and state to them the needs of the Lord's work and ask them to give to it."

So was Taylor exercising more faith by not asking? Or was Moody showing more faith by approaching people for money?

We need to be careful not to build our theology, philosophy and practice just based around great heroes of the faith, whether they asked or didn't ask. We need to build our foundation around the principles of scripture. And there is one passage in particular that is worth exploring that shows both Taylor and Moody were right!

Elijah's story

Take a look at 1 Kings 17. At the start of the chapter Elijah confronts Ahab, Israel's most ungodly leader to date. King, Ahab considered himself to be the supreme power in the land, so Elijah decided to show him who had the real power. He announced to Ahab that by the power of the God of Israel (as opposed to just the *King* of Israel) it wouldn't rain again until Elijah said it would. Ahab wasn't best pleased with this challenge to his authority, so life for Elijah suddenly became dangerous.

In verse two, God tells Elijah to hide in the Kerith Ravine and says that he will survive by drinking from the brook and eating food brought by ravens. And it didn't just happen by chance: God tells Elijah that he has *ordered* the birds to take care of him. So Elijah was able to survive thanks to these very unusual special gifts.

But Elijah had told Ahab that it wouldn't rain. So what happened to the stream? This vital source of Elijah's supply dried up. God could have made the empty brook fill with water as easily as he had arranged for the birds to feed Elijah, but for some reason he doesn't choose to continue with this type of unusual provision.

Instead he tells Elijah to go to Zarephath, a village well north and west of where Elijah was hiding that wasn't even part of Israel. God tells him that he has *commanded* a widow there to take care of him. When God had ordered the ravens to take care of him, the provision had simply appeared – Elijah didn't have to ask or even explain his needs to anyone.

Now God has *commanded* the widow to take care of him. So Elijah heads off to find this special provision that God has already prepared for him.

As he approaches the village he sees the widow gathering sticks for a fire. First of all he asks her for a drink of water and then, as an additional request, could she also bring him a piece of bread. The water she could get from the village well, but the bread was a different matter. It would have to come from her own resources – and she has just enough oil and flour left to make one last meal for herself and her son, and then they will die. So she turns down Elijah's request – it just isn't possible.

But God has already told Elijah that he has commanded this woman to take care of him. Unlike the same command to the ravens, this one doesn't seem to be so straightforward. The negative circumstances surrounding the widow are so contrary to God's call that she can't hear the command, let alone respond to it, and even if she wanted to help, there is no way she could.

So how does this man of God respond to her refusal to care for him?

First of all he tells this woman with only enough food for one last meal not to be afraid – probably a good idea, given what he's going to tell her next! He then tells her to make some bread for him first. Only after that, he says, can she make a meal for herself and her son. So with this tiny bit of food, barely enough for her and her young boy, she is now supposed to feed this grown man first. He ends his request with a promise that, if she does as he asks, God will meet her needs in a miraculous way until the rains come again and she will be able to provide for herself once more.

The woman does as Elijah asks, using her last resources to feed him first, and it turns out just as Elijah had said. Miraculously, she has enough oil and flour every day to keep her going until the rains come.

> God gives us situations where we need to ask. It isn't our choice whether or not we should ask, it's God's choice.

At the start of the story we see Elijah being provided for in an unusual way, with no asking and no one but God aware of his need. Maybe Hudson Taylor was right.

Then we see Elijah not only making his needs known to the widow, but asking her to meet the need. And when she says that she can't help him, he doesn't accept her 'no' as an appropriate answer and asks her a second time, insisting that she use her last provision for his benefit. Maybe D.L. Moody was right.

What can be learnt?

So, what lessons can we learn from this story?

First of all, it is not suggested that we take the last penny from every widow we meet! Nor that we don't accept someone's decision not to support us. But there are some key points about support-raising in this story.

God chooses how our support works

Sometimes His plan involves support arriving from apparently strange sources without our asking. Sometimes His plan involves us making our needs known to people and asking for their support. In this story both happened to Elijah immediately after each other, with no apparent reason for the change. We don't have the freedom to let our preferences, emotions or abilities be the deciding factor in whether or not we ask for support.

Throughout your ministry there are likely to be instances where God chooses to provide without us asking, but at other times God might give you situations where you need to ask. Both Taylor and Moody were right. But it isn't their choice whether or not you should ask. Nor is it our choice, or even yours. It is God's choice.

We need to keep talking to God about our support
It was God's instruction to go to the widow that gave Elijah the confidence not only to approach her, but also to ask again after she turned him down. If Elijah had just been acting by his own reasoning, he might not have approached her at all and he probably wouldn't have asked a second time after she said no, and the widow and her son would have died. It isn't a case of asking or praying. We always need to pray, whether or not we ask.

Sometimes the person receiving the support needs to have faith for both themselves and the person being asked

It wasn't until some time later in the story that the widow understood that Elijah was God's man.

God might create a set of connections and circumstances where your need to receive is the trigger required to help another person recognise their need to give

It might feel strange, it might involve direct asking, it might include discussion about the person's response and it might feel uncomfortable, but it shouldn't be our levels of discomfort that determine whether we encourage someone to discover a call of God on their lives.

We don't know why the other person needs to give but we do know that God blesses giving

In this story Elijah is quite specific about what this blessing will look like. It is unusual for us to have such insight and it can sound like spiritual blackmail to tell someone that God's blessing will follow their giving. But even if we don't explain it, we know from Jesus' own words that blessing follows giving, even if the potential supporter isn't aware of it. In this case the blessing to the widow and her son was that their lives were saved. What if Elijah had chosen not to pursue his request for her support?

> God might create a set of connections and circumstances where your need to receive is the trigger required to help another person recognise their need to give.

In the end, neither Elijah nor the widow are the central characters in this story. God is at the heart of it, arranging connections between two people, one with a need to receive and one with a need to give. Elijah was well aware of his need to receive but the widow wasn't aware of her need to give. It took a strange set of circumstances engineered by God to bring both needs to the surface. Elijah needed to have faith for both of them and it was by asking the widow to give him food that the call on her life was awakened.

The provision through the ravens without asking and the provision through the widow with asking are both expressions of God's grace and they are both expressions of Elijah's faith. It's not up to us to decide how it works: it is up to God. And that might mean being willing to ask in situations where our emotions will make it a challenge to do so. We need to let God's word be our guide, not our emotions.

Elijah – a man just like us

It's easy to read a story like this and say, "Yes, but that was Elijah. He was a prophet of God. It was okay for him to respond like this, but not me." Not true. When talking about Elijah's relationship with God in terms of his prayer life, James tells us: 'Elijah was a man just like us.' (James 5:17) You and I are no different today from what Elijah was back then – someone with material needs that need to be met to allow us to fulfil God's call on our lives. All of us are fully dependent on God and, like Elijah, we need to follow how he leads in the process. And it might be down some unexpected paths – maybe even more unexpected for the supporter than for you!

For reflection and/or discussion on Chapter 3

1. Which position do you agree with the most when it comes to divine provision?
   - Mission pioneer Hudson Taylor who said: "God's work, done God's way, will never lack God's supply", or
   - D.L. Moody, the American evangelist who said: "I show my faith when I go to men and state to them the needs of the Lord's work and ask them to give to it."
2. What is it about your experience that causes you to think this?
3. How open are you to seeing both methods of provision work out for you?

Notes

Being a good receiver/steward

AAA rating!

In the finance industry there is a commonly used rating system that assesses financial institutions and products where the 'top rating' gives an entity a 'triple A rating' or 'AAA'. Christian ministries similarly get assessed, normally informally and often unconsciously. These assessments should not be based on the world's financial judgments but on biblical values.

The Apostle Paul sets out these values in 2 Corinthians chapters 8 and 9 regarding the 'Jerusalem offering' and each can be handily summarised using words beginning with the letter 'A', thereby creating a biblical 'AAA' rating. The stronger our biblical AAA rating, the better receiver we will be. So what are these three As?

> Financial supporters want to be involved more than simply at the level of their wallets, they want to be engaged with their heart and soul too.

A is for advocacy

As you progress on this journey, you will link-in with many others. We always advise that you set up an inner core "support and accountability group" (see chapter 5) with which you are able to share most things, allowing them to speak into your life.

Secondly, you will attract a number of financial supporters, a sub-set of a larger group that will take more than a passing interest in what you are doing, and finally a wider friendship group that will consist of other church contacts, family and friends that will be interested in what you are doing and may perhaps pray for you, or support you in other ways.

Each group is different but for many that are not called to this type of ministry and lifestyle, hearing from you about what God is doing shows that you value them and is a source of encouragement, elevating the financial supporter to the status of a true partner with you. Being passionate about the work that you are involved in; sharing how it is making a difference to those who you are serving and explaining the impact of what you are doing for Christ's kingdom are all vital elements of that encouragement.

Financial supporters need (and sometimes want) to be involved more than simply at the level of their wallets; they want to be engaged practically and with their heart and soul too. Remember that the call for them to be 'sending' supporters is as real and relevant as your call to go, and this call extends well beyond the simple provision of financial resources. Like you, it is a call to make a difference.

It is important to stress that communication rests at the centre of true partnership and increasing the amount of time spent communicating with each of these groups will always be time well spent. We often hear comments from supporters such as: "I will be stopping my giving to support the ministry of X – you know I havent heard from them for years". This is borne out in surveys where 20% of Christian workers were found to spend less than two hours a month communicating with supporters. At the other end of the spectrum, another 20% spend around two days a month communicating with supporters.

Although some workers say, "I can't possible spend much time doing that I am far too busy", more experienced workers reflect differently saying "I can't possibly *not* spend significant time sharing with my ministry partners, my supporters – they are the life blood of my work".

In addition, around 20% of workers commented that they found it difficult to make new contacts, that they lacked courage, or that they simply did not consider that their needs carried sufficient value. Many also did not feel equipped to be able to get the message across. Creative use of the internet or social media can play a part here as can asking your contact groups to introduce you to others who may share your values and may want to enter into partnership with you. Taking opportunities to speak about your work whilst back with your UK church may also open some new doors.

Rest assured that other Christians will be interested in hearing what you have to say. They will be interested in what God is doing through your work and whether they feel called to support you financially or not, you will be a rich source of encouragement.

> Good administration helps good gospel work, whereas poor administration is often a significant barrier that impacts whether people see a ministry as 'worth supporting'.

A is for administration

In 2 Corinthians 8:19 the offering is described both as an 'administration of grace' and an activity which is 'to the glory of the Lord'. There is no disconnect between spirituality and governance. The structures by which we administer finances are established to enable our ministries to be an outworking of grace. Financial stewardship and administration is closely linked to the mission purpose.

Good administration helps good gospel work, whereas poor administration is a barrier often having a significant impact on whether people see a ministry as being 'worth supporting'. Demonstrating good administration is often as simple as:

> Healthy and informative dialogue is an encouragement to both partners.

- A commitment to communicate well with each 'contact group'. Communication is at the centre of true partnership and healthy and informative dialogue is an encouragement to both partners as they seek to fulfil God's calling on their lives. By requiring at least 10% of time to be spent communicating with supporters, Interserve recognise the crucial role that all supporters have to the success of your ministry.

- Keeping a record of income and expenditure. In this regard a ministry is similar to a business; there needs to be good basic 'book-keeping'. You certainly don't need to employ an accountant but knowing what money has come in and from where, and what money has gone out and how it has been spent is an important feature of sustainable ministry, not least as it allows you to understand whether your income and expenditure is in line with what you were expecting.

- Dealing correctly with taxation. Taxation can be complex, but for most it will in some form be inevitable. In this regard you need to understand certain things; your tax status and whether you are self-employed; your taxation responsibilities (if any) to the country in which you are serving; Interserve's responsibility for your tax affairs including what they can help with and what they can't. For some, it may be appropriate to take up to date and tailored professional advice before embarking on this route or at times when tax returns and payments are due.

- Thoughtful financial management. This includes simple budgeting, saving, being free from debt, and having the right insurance where necessary. These things are not in conflict with faith or our reliance on God to meet out needs. Some workers may argue, "but I trust God for my finances– so these things are not needed or even right for my ministry". In response, an appropriate analogy might be of Christians who drive cars at night; they may trust God for their safety but they still turn their lights on!

- One area that continues to grow in prominence is that of student debt. Many people do not realise that when working abroad, repayment of the debt 'kicks in' at a much lower income threshold than for people working in the UK. A failure to plan for this will divert funds away from your ministry, perhaps limiting what it can achieve.

A is for accountability

It is important that those who receive funds are accountable for their use. Not at a detailed micro level of having to justify every item of expenditure, but at a broad directional level. Transparency, integrity and timeliness are the watch words here.

First and foremost we are all accountable to God. He is our provider and it is to Him that we will ultimately answer. But beyond God there are others to whom you may be considered accountable:

- Your church: Flawed but still the body of Christ and an important instrument of advancing Christ's kingdom on earth.

- Your dependants and/or spouse: Dependent children or other relatives. The Bible makes it clear that we have responsibilities to our family that are equally as important as our ministry.

- Your support and accountability group (see chapter 5): This is a group of good friends who value you and believe in what you are doing that provide encouragement, wisdom, protection and honesty.

> Interserve require that at least 10% of work/ministry time is spent communicating with supporters.

- Your other ministry partners. This will include Interserve, your financial supporters (both individual and grant making trusts) and extends to others who support you in other ways.

Accountability sometimes carries with it negative connotations of control. Used wrongly, this can indeed be the case, but at its best accountability is liberating often allowing space for evaluation and changes in direction as the Holy Spirit leads and encourages. Financial accountability means talking about money (a most un-British trait), explaining your situation and often asking for support. This is best achieved in that spirit of openness, transparency and integrity mentioned earlier and those discussions will help to build deeper bonds between supporter and recipient for the benefit of both and to the glory of God.

Following through with your own AAA rating; having good administration; being accountable and being a strong advocate will serve you well as you work out God's calling on your life and the financial responsibilities and implications that will inevitable accompany that call.

Some financial responsibilities when living on a support basis

Does someone living on a support basis in Christian ministry live by different financial rules than a Christian in any other walk of life?

The Bible talks a lot about how we should handle money and material goods. Jesus dealt with this topic more than any other during his ministry but we find little or no specific principles in scripture that indicate that mission workers should view money any differently from others. How God gets his resources into the hands of those who raise support may differ from how he gets his resources into the hand of others, but the ultimate owner and provider of the money is God, irrespective of how it gets to us. We are all accountable to God for how we use the resources He gives us.

> People who can help provide good administration, accountability and strong advocacy, will all serve you well as you work out God's calling on your life.

There are however, common (albeit incorrect) *perceived* differences, with comments like 'living by faith' used for mission workers, somehow implying that a Christian teacher, civil servant, office worker, check-out operator or bank official lacks some faith in how they live. As discussed earlier, there can also be an assumption on the part of both the supporter and the mission partner that the full-time Christian worker lives on God's money and so has higher obligations on how it is used compared to the supporter who supposedly lives on his 'own' money.

The shift in mindset that is required is best illustrated by this quote from an overseas mission worker.

'The hardest part of living on a support basis as an overseas worker was the switch in mind-set that it required! After being brought up to work hard, to get a good job in order to be financially independent I was now in a position where I was having to ask people to give me money to do the work that I felt God was calling me to. Getting some good biblical input regarding the stewardship of my own possessions was really helpful. However, it was a cup of coffee, bought for me by a financially struggling friend who reminded me that all our money "comes from the same pot" that revolutionised my thinking.'

'Yours O LORD, is the greatness and the power and the glory and the majesty and the splendour, for everything in heaven and earth is yours…wealth and honour come from you.' (1 Chrons.29:11,12) If I was going to ask people for financial support I had to develop a different attitude towards my own possessions. As I gave more, and was blessed by doing so, the biblical truth that *'it is more blessed to give than to receive'* (Acts 20:35) became a reality in my life that I wanted others to experience too.

So while there are no differences in the basic principles that guide both Christian workers and supporters on their attitude to, and use of, money, there can be some emotional differences brought about by incorrect perceptions. There are also some practical differences resulting from living on a support basis which are explored further in chapter 7 – practical guidance and tips.

> 'It is more blessed to give than to receive.'
> (Acts 20:35)

Issues in short-term mission

If you are only going into mission for a couple of years there may not be many significant financial implications. You may need to consider whether to pay a voluntary National Insurance contribution (depending on your employment status and location), whether to rent out your home or review some investments and outgoings to see if any amendments are needed for the time you are in mission. Nevertheless, a couple of years in mission won't make a huge difference to how you organise your long-term finances, assuming you are already operating as best you can according to the basic principles God has given us in scripture.

There may, of course, be implications for your career such as whether your job will remain open until you return or how easy it might be to find something similar on your return. You may risk missing out on promotion in your absence but conversely you may improve your career prospects by demonstrating that you are willing to take the initiative and tackle a challenge. This is not so much a risk assessment as an evaluation of the true cost.

Finally, remember following God's call is about His glory, not about our job security. So even if your decision to respond to His call to be involved in mission for a short time results in you not getting the career advancement you had hoped for, is that really such a big deal? If we want to hear well done good and faithful servant, we need to serve God faithfully and to the best of our ability – that's all.

Longer-term mission

If, however, God has called you to several years in supported Christian ministry, you will need to do some serious thinking. First of all you will need to consider how you handle the legal obligations of your financial status as a mission partner. For example, being sure about your tax status. Just because you are a mission partner living on support doesn't mean you are exempt from paying taxes in the country you serve in.

Recent policy changes in a number of European countries have resulted in mission workers who thought they were exempt from local taxes having to pay back taxes retrospectively. Get good advice and don't assume that a discussion that you heard that someone had with a government official some years ago has any legal bearing.

> God may choose to meet a future need in advance, remember Joseph's actions in the years of abundance in Genesis 41:46-49

As well as sorting out how to render to Caesar what Caesar requires (or at least his modern-day equivalent), you will need to ask, and answer, some questions about how you will provide for yourself and your family in the short, medium and long-term.

For some, there is a perceived conflict between a reliance on God and thinking about longer-term needs. Whilst such a conflict is largely illusory, the longer-term needs like housing, living costs in old age, life insurance etc, are all too real and should be addressed early in life to avoid those difficulties that will inevitably emerge later (which, regardless of your current age, is closer than you might think).

God may choose to meet a future need in advance, remember Joseph's actions in the years of abundance in Genesis 41:46-49, and these same principles still apply today. In the years when you have money available and when your supporters are still working and able to give, it is appropriate to set some money aside to help cover the costs of later life when your supporters' ability to give financially is likely to be reduced.

So thinking and planning ahead about these issues make sense. Each person will have a different approach to these issues and your family background, lifestyle choices, possible future family inheritance etc, will help shape the approach you take. As long as you are comfortable under God about your choices and as long as you can effectively respond to Paul's comment to Timothy that those who do not take care of their immediate family have denied the faith and are worse than unbelievers (1Tim.5:8) - that in itself should be enough to scare you into action on this. Whatever you do, don't bury your head in the sand and don't wait until it is too late to do something about it. Today is always a good day to start planning realistically for the future.

For reflection and/or discussion on Chapter 4

1. If the call for 'sending' supporters is as real and relevant as your call to go, what practical steps could you take to enable your financial supporters to be involved more than simply at the level of their wallets?

2. Make sure that you thought through properly, how long your full-time involvement in misison might be?

3. How realistic do you think it is to ask that workers budget at least 10% of their working time to be spent communicating with supporters? How might you go about this – starting now?

Notes

How much is enough?

Whilst serving with Interserve you will receive an allowance to meet the costs of sending and supporting you in your country of service. This does not however mean that the question 'how much is enough?' is irrelevant. It is a question that pre-dates Jesus, and it isn't just a question for mission workers or 'Christian workers'. In Proverbs 30:7-9 we read:

'Two things I ask of you, Lord; do not refuse me before I die: Keep falsehood and lies far from me; give me neither poverty nor riches, but give me only my daily bread. Otherwise, I may have too much and disown you and say, 'Who is the Lord?' or I may become poor and steal, and so dishonour the name of my God.'

Paul says to Timothy: 'If anyone does not provide for his relatives, and especially for his immediate family, he has denied the faith and is worse than an unbeliever.'
(1Tim.5:8)

If we have much more financial support than we need we can become complacent and lose sight of God as our provider. But if we have much less than we need, while we mightn't resort to theft, we may be tempted to take back control of our provision from God, become anxious and do things our way without reference to what God wants us to do.

So how much is enough? It can depend on what ministry God has called you to, how many dependants you have, what debt you may be carrying from the past, whether you need to cover your ministry costs as well as your basic living costs, your family lifestyle choices, whether you have independent resources to help cover costs when you and your supporters are much older, how long you are planning to live on a support basis and many other factors.

In this section we aren't setting out to answer the question, 'how much is enough?' What we are trying to do is offer some biblical guidelines along with practical suggestions to help you ask the right questions of yourself. As there are many more Christian workers at the 'not enough' end of the spectrum rather than at the 'too much' end, the comments are slanted in that direction.

Some of these biblical principles may seem to sit awkwardly alongside some of the others, but they all form part of God's word on the issue. Each was written or spoken in a specific context that is unlikely to be the same as yours, but do what you can to bring your life onto the foundation that these principles offer. Of course there are many more passages we could look at, so please add the results of your own study to the ones we've chosen.

Before we look at these, just a reminder of why this is important. Some of the most materialistic people we have ever met are mission workers with low support – their minds are consumed with material issues, sometimes even worrying where the next meal is coming from. Guilt can also kick in with questions like: "Shouldn't I be able to live more frugally?", "Shouldn't I be able to trust God more for my provision?", "Maybe my ministry isn't really worth supporting" and "Who am I to enjoy luxuries in life?"

> what's the purpose then of accumulating a pile of material goods that we can't take with us?

The consequences of this type of thinking can be many: fear for their family's future, loss of joy, worrying about where the next meal is coming from, distraction from the work God has called them to, reduced effectiveness in their work for God because they have minimum money and sometimes stepping out of God's primary calling on their lives because they didn't have enough.

Whose fault is it? Is it the fault of the supporters who should have given more? Maybe, but then mission workers aren't always that good, or comfortable, about communicating their needs. So we can't lay all the blame on the supporter. As the mission community, we need to take responsibility ourselves as far as possible to make the right decisions and do the right things in resourcing God's call on our lives.

The principles

So, let's look at the principles:

You have a responsibility to your family

In 1Timothy 5:8 Paul says to Timothy, If anyone does not provide for his relatives, and especially for his immediate family, he has denied the faith and is worse than an unbeliever. The immediate context is talking about the caring for elderly relatives, but the foundational principle is that God expects you to care for those he has entrusted to you. The consequences of not doing so are serious. An experienced mission worker who has led support seminars used to start by saying that there were five reasons he raised support. Then he would pass round a photo of his wife and four children and read aloud 1Timothy 5:8.

Don't get caught up with asset accumulation

In the very next chapter Paul says, *But if we have food and clothing we will be content with that* (1Tim. 6:8). He makes this comment in contrast to those who *think that godliness is a means of financial gain* (6:5) so he is making a strong point to those who were hoping that their commitment to Christian faith would bring them material wealth.

Given that *we brought nothing into this world and we can take nothing out of it* (6:7) his point seems to be, what's the purpose then of accumulating a pile of material goods that we can't take with us? Paul's main argument in this section from 6:3-10 is that if you want to pursue godliness you cannot love money. He doesn't say that money is bad, but rather that the pursuit and love of money causes you to be distracted from following God.

However, unnecessary and undesirable asset accumulation should not be confused with sensible long-term thinking. As you get older so will many of your financial supporters. Their situations will change and it is likely that their ability to give financially will be reduced. If you have not planned for this, or provided in the future, your older life might be less than comfortable and the fruitfulness of your ministry may be curtailed earlier than is necessary.

Don't worry

Much of Matthew 6 is given over to how we respond to worry about money. It is interesting to note that immediately after Jesus' comment that you cannot serve God and Mammon, he says: *Therefore I tell you, do not worry about your life, what you will eat or drink; or about your body, what you will wear* (Matt.6:24-25). This whole passage says that we have a choice. We can serve God, in which case we shouldn't worry about material goods or we can serve Mammon, in which case we will worry about material goods.

He was willing to go with the flow of the resources that were available to him at any given time.

Put God's kingdom first

Near the end of Matthew 6, Jesus tells the disciples that their primary focus should be on God: *Seek first his kingdom and his righteousness, and all these things will be added to you as well* (6:33).

Yes, we need to take our support seriously;

Yes, we need to do what we can to provide for our families;

Yes, we are called to the work of the King of Kings and need to give the resourcing of that task our best attention.

But in the end, we focus on God's kingdom and his righteousness. Our trust is in him. He is our provider, not our supporters. And as we live out the reality of this in the light of our support target, we should do all that we can to ensure that we have the support we need, confident that he will do all that we can't do.

Those who start something they can't finish will look stupid

In illustrating the need to be sure you are aware of the cost of following him, Jesus tells the story of a man who started to build a tower but ran out of money before he could finish it. It made him look stupid. (Lk.14:28-29). So when deciding how much is enough, it is important to factor in expenses that you may be tempted to leave out to keep your support need seemingly lower.

> None of this is deserved by us and all of it is bought for us on the cross. What a privilege!

Being able to have a family holiday, changing a car when needed, continuing to live at a realistic level when your supporters are retired or dead, paying for the future education of your children and similar expenses are realities, so funding for these should be included in the amount you raise over the long term. Otherwise you might end up not being able to pay for some critical expenses that could have been anticipated at an earlier stage.

As Interserve move from standard budgets to personalised budgets, these issues become more pertinant.

Is it okay to pursue a hobby or to go to a nice restaurant to celebrate your anniversary? Is it okay to raise support for pension contributions? As long as you are comfortable under God with your choices, then these expenses are fine. The discomfort we experience is caused when we forget that the money we receive belongs to God and not to our supporters. Then we will start basing our actions and financial lifestyle on what our supporters might think, or more accurately on what we think our supporters might think!

Paul was content with whatever situation he was in

Paul tells his supporters in Philippi: *I have learned the secret of being content in any and every situation, whether being well fed or hungry, whether living in plenty or in want* (Phils.4:12). He had clearly lived in plenty and also in want, but he didn't say that one was better than the other. He was willing to go with the flow of the resources that were available to him at any given time, sometimes a lot, sometimes not. But Paul didn't appear to have any family dependent on him and his calling was to a travelling, itinerant ministry, not a life settled in one place. Did that make this comment easier for him?

God gives us things to enjoy

Following on from the last one, peace or enjoyment is one of the tests of good decisions. 1Timothy 6:17 talks about *God, who richly provides everything for our enjoyment..* and many of the Psalms emphasise the abundance and tender goodness of God. This is not to say there will not be seasons, as there were clearly for Paul, when being 'in want' was the experience, but if there is a long-term nag of discontentment or 'lack' then this is a warning sign that should not be ignored.

You are a prince or princess in the family of the King of Kings

Peter tells us that we are *a chosen people, a royal priesthood, a holy nation, a people belonging to God, that you may declare the praises of him who called you out of darkness into his wonderful light* (1Pt.2:9-10). None of this is deserved by us and all of it is bought for us on the cross. What a privilege!

You are a prince or princess in God's kingdom, with all the privileges of that position, with the riches of his glory lavished on us (Eph.1:8), and with a request from the King of Kings to work for him to explain to other people how they can come into his wonderful light. So why, in this massively important task, do we so often ask ourselves "what's the least I can raise and still survive?" instead of, "what is a realistic amount of resources that I need to do this task to the absolute best of my ability?"

As said at the beginning, there are no clear answers and each person will interpret these points differently, depending on your own situation, adding points from other passages. That's fine, so long as it is God's word you are building on, not your own emotions or fears; not the preconceived ideas of supporters about how mission workers should live and not a limited view of God's abundant resources for his work.

Remember, whether you are a mission partner with an income from supporters or a supporter with an income from an employer, God is the provider for everyone and these principles apply equally to both. However, sometimes those who live from others' gifts can feel under pressure because they think they are living on supporters' money. They aren't – they, like the supporters, are living on God's money and it is his principles that need to guide them, not the expectations of the supporters.

For reflection and/or discussion on Chapter 5

The following questions and statements are likely to occur to you at some stage in your mission involvement. How do you think you will handle them if and when they crop up?

1. "Shouldn't I be able to live more frugally?"

2. "Shouldn't I be able to trust God more for my provision?"

3. "Maybe my ministry isn't really worth supporting"

4. "Who am I to enjoy luxuries in life?"

Notes

Culture change and support groups

The reality for most people that travel from the UK to overseas mission fields is that this will be their first experience of seeing for themselves the wealth and affluence imbalance that exists on our planet. Many might be intellectually aware of this imbalance, via the UK media, but this is very differnet from experiencing the sights, sounds and smells first hand.

Whilst the desire to preach the gospel lies at the root of most mission calling, the impact of what you will see and experience should not be underestimated, and will undoubtedly have a profound impact on the way that you go about your work and perhaps even the way that you seek to raise funds.

The obvious anomalies between the affluent and the poor have been around for centuries and were addressed brilliantly, more than twenty years ago in the book *Missions and Money* by Jonathan Bonk.[2]

He describes well the respective contextual and historical arguments both for and against the presumption that after the industrial revolution, it is the affluent colonial believer who – while retaining his new found wealth – aspires and activates his calling to share the gospel with those to whom wealth is a distant dream.

> We are called to share the gospel and disciple the nations, wherever 'we' are from and wherever 'the nations' may be.

Perhaps we can never know the answer to the ooming conundrum of western affluence, money and mission, but we do know that whatever the believer's circumstances, we are called to share the gospel and disciple the nations, wherever 'we' are from and wherever 'the nations' may be – overseas or dispersed in the West.

God does not ask the size of our bank balance before we set out on a mission path; both rich and poor alike are called to serve Him in this way. He is the provider and has no need for our wealth. What we do know is that He does expect obedience to His calling, not least to the hungry, the thirsty, the naked and the imprisoned:

---

2   *Jonathan J. Bonk*, Mission and Money – affluence as a missionary problem revisited, *Orbis Books, 2006*

"Whatever you did for one of the least of these brothers and sisters of mine, you did for me"

So although affluence is not the issue (indulgence of course may be but that's another issue) and our heart for the 'spiritually poor' continues to be the primary motive for mission, to ignore the impact that seeing this imbalance firsthand will have is perhaps naive.

For many people, seeing lifestyles and the level of deprivation that is so different from anything they have experienced previously, will trigger in them a desire to see the sort of social justice and reform Jesus spoke of. It may also trigger in some, a sense of confusion and guilt for the way they have previously lived in the UK as well as an uncertainty as to how they should live in their current situation. These feelings are both natural and to be expected.

Support groups will be your 'inner-circle' to support you in your calling.

This cultural uncertainty and friction may show itself in many guises. These give rise to general philosophoical questions such as: "Just how much is enough?" (see chapter 5), or else specific questions such as the following:

- *"How closely should I integrate with the host culture?"*
  Interserve expects its misison partners to engage fully with the culture of their host country or community. We provide orientation both prior to leaving and from arrival onwards. Where necessary, the first year (sometimes two) of the eassignment includes language learning. So as well as the prior orientation by those who already have experience in a particular culture and/or religion, this is enhanced 'in country' by those who are already there.

- *"Should I have access to medical and other insurances?"*
  Interserve believes in taking all appropriate measures to ensure adequate insurance, and will certainly work with the Partner to achieve this, prior to the Partner heading overseas. This includes medical insurance.

- *"What about education for my children?"*
  Interserve recognises the calling on families to serve overseas and therefore the resulting requirements of academic education for their children. For those travelling overseas, there are three options: 1. an international (private) school: 2. a school for mission children and 3. home schooling. All three have both advantages and drawbacks but academic education is a necessity, and Interserve advises in this area.

- *"Is it still OK to spend money on western style goods?"*

  The economic-divide is part of cross-cultural mission. Aim at a balance between flaunting comparative wealth and artificial poverty (locals will spot that too). In the fourth booklet in this series, Martin Goldsmith says: "We are called to share the same predicament as others. Then we can point people to Jesus without appearing arrogant." The simple rule is that authentic witness to Jesus is 'incarnational'.

This helps guide us through issues such as the social strata of people we are living among so we can pitch our lifestyle, dress and possessions accordingly. We should not overdo it in either direction because ultimately people know where we are from.

> You may be plunged into an affluence-gap perhaps wondering how and why resources and wealth appear to be so unevenly distributed.

When returning to your regular life in the UK, either as a break or permanently – depending upon how long you have spent engaged in cross-cultural mission – many of the same feelings will perhaps emerge again in what we call "reverse culture-shock". You may be plunged into an affluence-gap perhaps wondering how and why resources and wealth appear to be so unevenly distributed. Often the re-acclimatisation to a more affluent lifestyle is just as difficult as the original transition overseas, and care and support may be required as you return to the UK.

It is important that any accountability and support group that you have in place (see next section) is not immediately disbanded but continues in place for as long as you need to allow time, space and support to find your place back in the UK – we recommend at least six months for every year spent outside your previous "normality".

What about support and accountability groups?

Support and accountability groups come in many shapes, but will be your 'inner-circle'. As the name suggests, their primary function is to support you and your family in your calling. They are essentially a group of good friends who both value you and are committed to you, believing wholeheartedly in what you are doing.

They are able to provide encouragement, wisdom, protection and can speak honestly and openly into your particular situation. It is important that these groups include people who are independently minded; have broad and different life experiences; have both you and the Kingdom's interests at heart and with whom you can have some fun. Try not to only include people who are 'just like you!'

It is difficult to overestimate the importance of these groups. One piece of advice from a person involved in long-term supported ministry for many years was "above all else do not lose your personal support group" – strong stuff. This was echoed by Lynn Green, UK Director of YWAM International, who commented that "Christian work is a lonely place" as he acknowledged the vital role that, for him and his wife Marty, his own personal support group had been to them in their ministry.

'At the beginning of our ministry we were often living hand to mouth and it felt quite stressful and lonely. At the suggestion of our friends we formed a smallish group to specifically support us in our ministry. For over 35 years we've been meeting two or three times a year. It is important to invest time and energy into these friendships, nurturing your support group is as important as your mission work. In turn they have enriched our lives and provided a stability and a refuge through difficult times.' Lynn Green, YWAM

Such meetings should be a high priority for both the worker and the supporters.

These groups provide essential prayer support; they may include financial supporters, and will act as advisers and guides providing both wise council and stability. They are not a legal board, and neither are they there as a replacement to your ultimate responsibility for your own decision, but used wisely such a group offers an array of long-term benefits which are difficult to access elsewhere.

Advance planning to meet together is essential, and such meetings should be a high priority for both the worker and the supporters. Whilst Skype is a useful tool, nothing beats 'face-to-face' contact allowing a relaxed and unhurried time to focus on the worker's situation; explore what God may be saying; discuss future direction; explaing needs and praying.

For reflection and/or discussion on Chapter 6

1. Give some thought to what you might be doing after your full-time mission experience. In what ways could you continue to be involved with the same people group you served among in a full-time capacity?

2. Reflect on Jonathan Bonk's analysis of the conundrum whereby comparatively affluent western Christians who – while retaining their 'wealth' – aspire to share the gospel with those to whom wealth is still a distant dream.

3. Have you seen abject poverty first hand? How do you think you will cope when living among people with such a massive economic-divide? Who will you turn to for guidance to distinguish between 'professional' and genuine beggars?

Practical guidance and tips

1. God has made us all different, so we will make different choices in many areas. As Paul outlines in Romans 14, we are called to give an account of ourselves to God and we are called to trust God and each other's relationship with Him with the consequence that we do not judge others by our choices and are not afraid of being judged by others. The exception to this would be acting outside of scriptural teaching in which case we do need to speak to each other clearly.

2. Being more open with your supporters will help. If supporters know your situation, they are better able to help make some of these decisions with you – if asked. Sometimes they might even make the decision for you as a way of sharing in the blessing of partnership with you. For example giving specifically in order to help you take, not just a 'well-earned break' but a more major and expensive holiday or to help fund retirement.

   > Even when supporters don't understand, make sure you communicate in a way that allows them into the privilege of involvomont.

   This transparency isn't the same as feeling obliged to disclose to your supporters every last penny you spend, which can lead to unhelpful thinking about having to get supporters' permission. In practice, a support or accountability group can be of real help in working through 'what is enough' as they can look more objectively at your needs. Remember: supporters aren't primarily about the money – their relationship is one of involvement and trust.

3. If you are married, talk to your spouse about your finances. At the risk of stereotyping, husbands can feel the pressure of being the provider and get confused when God doesn't seem to provide what the family needs. So they can revert to 'don't worry, God will provide' and not actually do anything about it. Meanwhile, the wife can face the challenge of buying food today without the luxury of saying to the person at the checkout: 'Don't worry, God will provide'.

   It's not that one approach is more correct; it can just be the result of viewing finance (or lack of it) from different perspectives. Be open and honest with each other and, if it helps, involve a trusted friend (possibly a support group?) to help you talk through your different perspectives.

4. Prepare a budget: every home should have one! Knowing what you spend your money on, and what you should be planning to spend money on, is a useful exercise. It gives an overview of your finances over the medium-term and can help you identify where money is needed, not just on a day-by-day basis. It isn't a tool that removes faith in God, but it is one that helps practical prioritisation of what we spend and sometimes it is the very exercise of budgeting that means we see what we need to do.

In constructing a budget – be realistic. Avoid the temptation to exclude costs that you know, or could reasonable expect, will occur just so that the amount that you need to raise is lower. Whilst there are some completely unexpected costs, most expenditure can be reasonably well anticipated if some thought is applied. It does not make you appear more spiritual to be always on the edge when you don't really need to be. It just makes you look disorganised and unplanned!

> Budgeting doesn't remove faith in God, it helps prioritisation. Sometimes just doing it means we can see what we need.

There are many ways a budget can be prepared[3] but if you would like a copy of Stewardship's practical budget tool specifically designed for Christian workers 'Painting by numbers for Christian workers' please contact education@stewardship.org.uk

5. Do not get into debt. It is easy to slip into but a nightmare to get out of. It is so easy to think that because there isn't the expected money now that somehow it will be there in the future – it can seem 'an easy way out'. By debt we mean an amount owed that you can't repay, or where you can't keep up with a planned schedule of repayments; such as a balance on a credit card, a couple of months late with house payments, unable to repay a loan to a friend, a deficit run up with your mission, Bible college fees still not all paid, money owed to the local Christian bookshop and so on.

With mission workers, debt doesn't usually happen because of wasteful spending, but rather because they underestimate how much they need or because they hope that, somehow, money will arrive when it is needed – it might not. The key to the first of these is to have a realistic budget that covers all expenses, not just the immediate daily costs, and includes an amount for unplanned emergencies. The key to the second is to raise enough regular support to cover the budget and not assume that money will just appear when a bill arrives. If you do get into debt, even a small amount, talk to somebody about it at the very start.

---

3   See www.stewardship.org.uk for BudgetBuilder online budgeting tool or search resources section for a paper-based budget sheet.

It is too easy to let it slide, hoping that it will somehow get sorted. Often all that gives you is more debt. Talk to someone in Interserve, your pastor or a trusted friend or support group. There are also some good Christian-based organisations who can advise you and Stewardship would be happy to talk to you.

6. If the amount Interserve says you will need is more than you think you need, believe them. Support targets set objectively are often a lot more realistic than one individuals might set for themselves. If you don't have anyone to guide you on how much you need, Stewardship would be more than willing to help you set a realistic support figure for your life and ministry.

7. Understand your tax situation. Taxation can be complex, but for most people it will be inevitable in some form. In this regard you need to understand certain things: your tax status and whether you are self-employed; your taxation responsibilities (if any) to the country in which you are serving; Interserve's responsibility for your tax affairs including what they can help with and what they can't. For some, it may be appropriate to take up-to-date and tailored professional advice before embarking on this route or at times when tax returns and payments are due.

8. Listen to your Interserve coach. The concept of coaching is very often linked with sports in people's minds but benefiting from it is not only an athlete's privilege. A coach's role is to help people accomplish their goals, which in this context is personal financial support raising. Bringing their expertise to bear, a coach will look to encourage in all areas, help dispel myths about money, offer biblical and practical insights, and offer support and accountability.

The process may involve some direct practical advice but more often than not there will be some careful and exploratory questioning in order to help identify a strategy that the recipient is comfortable with. The coach will also set realistic and achievable targets for action, acknowledging and building on the strength of past achievements.

9. Think about retirement. All too often, difficulties emerge as workers approach retirement with little or no pension provision. Some are not even sure whether they will be able to claim the full state pension which is dependent upon the payment of National Insurance over a long period of time (currently 30 years to qualify for the full state pension, although this may be increasing to 35 years). Whilst serving overseas with Interserve, they will pay Voluntary Development Worker (VDW) class 2 National Insurance contributions on your behalf as long as you are under retirement age, but it may be worth checking your National Insurance record and voluntarily making up for years that you might have missed where possible.

While serving with Interserve you will be able to apply to join the Global Connections (i.e. Evangelical Missionary Alliance - EMA) *Money Purchase Plan* into which Interserve will make regular monthly payments to provide for a future pension. There is nothing to stop either yourself, or your supporters from making additional payments should you consider this appropriate. It is always sad when those who are older and with years of experience are unable to share their valuable experience with others because they are limited by a lack of funds. Planning for this now will ensure your continued fruitfulness well into older age.

10. Home ownership. One mission agency had an older couple who were talked about in hushed tones in the mission where they had served for many years. After a few decades of faithful service overseas they had retired back to the UK and they spoke at a mission conference. They were asked what advice they would give to a young couple going into mission today, and answer was surprising - *buy a house before you go!*

It became clear from their explanation that they weren't advocating property purchase for its own sake, nor were they wanting just to live in comfort. They had gone overseas in the 1960s without any thought for the future and during their years abroad they had raised just enough to cover their daily needs. With no provision for their senior years, and with their financial support network reducing (due to retirement and death of supporters), they were now back in the UK and obliged to use a large percentage of their meagre income to rent an apartment. That left them without enough money to travel to other parts of the country to encourage Christians living in Britain but originally from the country they had served in for so long.

> They were asked what advice they would give to a young couple going into mission today, and answer was surprising - buy a house before you go!

If they had only made some provision for their future when their supporters were able to give, then they would have had enough money to continue serving the people God had called them to work with all those years ago.

11. There will be challenges. In Christian ministry funded on a personal support basis, much of what may be provided by an employer in a 'normal' job is likely to fall on you. You might need to fund your own pension plan, there may not be an annual pay rise, you might need to look after your own tax and national insurance affairs, promotion may not bring more money and you may well be expected to cover your own business costs. Given that the probability that the amount a Christian worker has for normal living expenses each month may well be lower than would be the case in other walks of life, there are undoubtedly financial challenges.

Conclusion/wrapping up

As you partner with agencies such as Interserve, you are embarking upon an exciting part of your life journey. One that God has called you to, and one that makes you a part of the rich heritage of people that God has sent out to bring his love, care, compassion and salvation to a needy world.

We hope that this booklet has helped you to see the role that money has as you seek to step out in the Lord's will. To help you remember that God is always the provider, and to give you some of the tools and insights that you will need as you move into serving Him in this new way.

One last observation; do not try to walk alone. Share your experiences, hopes and fears with those at Interserve who will be delighted to walk with you.

Further Reading:

Jonathan J. Bonk, *Mission and Money – affluence as a missionary problem revisited* (Orbis Books)

Interserve resources